Better Homes and Gardens®

# DECORATING WITH PERSONAL STYLE

**BETTER HOMES AND GARDENS® BOOKS**
Editor: Gerald M. Knox
Art Director: Ernest Shelton
Managing Editor: David A. Kirchner
Editorial Project Managers: James D. Blume,
    Marsha Jahns, Rosanne Weber Mattson,
    Mary Helen Schiltz

Senior Furnishings Editor, Books: Gayle Butler

Associate Art Directors: Neoma Thomas,
    Linda Ford Vermie, Randall Yontz
Assistant Art Directors: Lynda Haupert,
    Harijs Priekulis, Tom Wegner
Graphic Designers: Mary Schlueter Bendgen,
    Mike Burns, Brian Wignall
Art Production: Director, John Berg;
    Associate, Joe Heuer;
    Office Manager, Michaela Lester

President, Book Group: Fred Stines
Vice President, General Manager: Jeramy Lanigan
Vice President, Retail Marketing: Jamie L. Martin
Vice President, Administrative Services:
    Rick Rundall

BETTER HOMES AND GARDENS® MAGAZINE
President, James A. Autry
Vice President, Editorial Director: Doris Eby
Executive Director, Editorial Services:
    Duane L. Gregg
Furnishings and Design Editor: Shirley Van Zante

MEREDITH CORPORATE OFFICERS
Chairman of the Board: E.T. Meredith III
President: Robert A. Burnett
Executive Vice President: Jack D. Rehm

DECORATING WITH PERSONAL STYLE
Editor: Pamela J. Wilson
Project Editor: Marsha Jahns
Editorial Project Manager: Mary Helen Schiltz
Graphic Designer: Jack Murphy
Contributing Graphic Designer:
    Lyne Neymeyer
Electronic Text Processor: Paula Forest

**P**ersonal style is that certain something that makes a room sing its own special song. Whether the song is romantic, jazzy, country, witty, moody, or softly sentimental, it is always sung with confidence, and often with glorious gusto. What is this "something" so essential to style? Simply said, it's you: your passions, your penchants, even your peculiarities. Shortchanged of your presence, a room doesn't sing; it sulks.

*Decorating with Personal Style* is a picture book of homes where the owners have deftly and decisively made their presence felt. Each house is a celebration of original thinking, and each proves that it's personality—not just money or good taste—that makes a room memorable and easy to love.

Is inhibition standing between you and personal style? Worry not. *Decorating with Personal Style* will help you over the hurdles. We'll show you how to relax the rules and furnish your place with aplomb. We'll arm you with hundreds of scheming ideas, and we'll provide plenty of encouragement along the way. Before you know it, your house will be singing as it should.

# CONTENTS

# AT HOME WITH STYLE

*Great designs are not accomplished without enthusiasm of some sort. It is the inspiration of everything great.*

Christian Nestell Bovee

*Agnes Bourne is an interior designer, house renovator, furniture designer, art collector, equestrian, and world traveler wrapped into one. Her house—a happy meeting ground of all of her interests— is as fun to get to know as she is.*

■

There's something for everyone in the aerie: intriguing art (the boat shell is sculpture, as is the dog), a stage for art shows and impromptu performances, a ceiling-mounted film projector and drop-down screen, and plenty of seating. The Springfield sign? It came from an abandoned railway station in England.

# STYLE À LA AGNES

Her grown children characterize her style as "fifty percent Japanese, forty percent Italian, and ten percent New York taxi driver." Agnes Bourne basically agrees with this description, but says "the percentages are slightly off." Family assessments aside, Agnes Bourne's style can't be pigeonholed. Her passions and preferences are so diverse and her talents so magical and many, that definition doesn't come easy. Suffice it to say, Agnes' look is personal—delightfully and disarmingly so.

■

**This remodeled four-story San Francisco house is where Agnes, her husband, Dr. Jim Luebbers, and their children reside.**

# STYLE
# À LA AGNES

Agnes' interest in art began at age three, when she took crayons to the walls of her bedroom. An avid aesthete ever since, she is not only a serious collector, but a friend and patron of many of California's finest contemporary artists.

"My theory about art," Agnes explains, "is that it must amuse and confuse you, jar you, and make you come back and look again and again." There's no question that Agnes adheres to her own philosophy. In her recently remodeled San Francisco house, art is everywhere, and much—if not most—of it stops people in their tracks. Case in point: the life-size horse sculpture in the living room, *below*. Designed by Montana artist Deborah Butterfield, the steel and pipe equine is a real showstopper, just as intrepid Agnes knew it would be.

■ **Living room seating pieces—all designed by Agnes—are placed in the round atop an heirloom Heriz rug.**

■ **It's not every living room that can accommodate a full-size horse sculpture, but art collector/equestrian Agnes Bourne removed two walls to make a home for this one.**

# STYLE À LA AGNES

lthough Agnes the remodeler is never at a loss for ideas, she expects her clients to be fully involved in the design process. Before remodeling her own house, she relied heavily on the participatory school of planning. "Everybody in the family got quizzed and quizzed on their feelings about the house and how they wanted to use it," she explains. The plan that evolved was an open, easygoing environment where all of the "public" spaces—living room, dining room/library, entry hall, and kitchen—are in full view of one another.

The kitchen, because it rated "most important" on everyone's priority list, was given a prominent position at the front of the house, with a view of San Francisco Bay. Explains Agnes, "The kitchen is not only the heart of our home, but the hub of our family life; we all love to cook, and we like to keep tabs on the comings and goings of others."

■

**In the kitchen, puffy white clouds on a blue-sky background keep San Francisco's oft-present fog at bay.**

■

**Avant "guard" dogs, sculpted by artist Jim Lawrence, are "look again" surprises at the entryway.**

In the dining room,
a slab of marble makes
an elegant topper for
the laminate-surfaced
table.

A huge mural titled "House" is the focal point of the family dining room. Executed by Bay Area artist Squeak Carnwath, the mural is a painted "celebration" of Agnes and Jim's wedding day, and all of the elements hold special meaning for the family. Ceiling spotlights are aimed on this and other artwork.

■ **A spray of spring flowers and a pair of carved elephants from India are teamed artistically for a centerpiece.**

At the far end of the dining room is a pleasant library that, prior to remodeling, was a small, separate room. Agnes jokes that this dining/library arrangement puts "reference material near at hand for dinner table arguments." Actually, the real reason the rooms were combined was to provide space for large dinner parties. Agnes and Jim entertain often, and with two large extension tables in place, 30 people easily can be seated.

The library's south-facing window seat is a favorite spot for reading. Furnishings here include an antique library table and an 18th-century Chinese bench. Heirloom Kilim carpets cover the cushions, and several old saddlebags serve as toss pillows.

■

**The Kilim carpets that cover the seat cushions once belonged to Agnes' grandfather.**

■

**It was Agnes' novel idea to meld the dining area with the small, but well-stocked, library.**

# STYLE
# À LA AGNES

The master bedroom is "furnished" with panoramic views of San Francisco Bay. One window, *below,* puts the Golden Gate Bridge in the picture, and another (not shown) takes in Alcatraz, the old prison island. Agnes and Jim, from the vantage point of their higher-than-usual bed, have an unimpeded view of this spectacular scenery.

The bed frame is a Bourne original: old door frames that have been distressed and given a crackle paint finish. Sheet yardage covers the down comforter and assorted pillows, and an old English leather hat box serves as an out-of-the-ordinary bedside table.

Lined on the window ledge, *below,* are "little favorite things that just got there," relates Agnes, adding, "It's souvenirs like these that give me a sense of place; remind me of places we've been as a family."

■
**The bedroom is simply furnished so as not to compete with the breathtaking views.**

■
**Following her own "art must amuse you" philosophy, Agnes purchased this zany chairside table from artist/craftsman Boyd Wright.**

# ALL THINGS BEAUTIFUL

Laurie Adams Warren is a compulsive collector. What started as an innocent interest in "all things wonderful" has become an "affliction" that can't be harnessed. "I find beautiful old things irresistible," says Laurie, "and it takes great self-control not to fill each inch of my house with treasures."

A quick glance around Laurie's glorious Connecticut home might prompt a smile at her notion of self-control, but never mind. Her compulsion for collecting has spawned a spirited decorating style that Laurie describes as "extraordinarily eclectic."

Indeed, to explore the big yellow house is to encounter a rich and intriguing blend of ingredients. Remnants of various collecting bents are everywhere, and one never knows what sort of exotic mélange awaits beyond each door. The foyer, *opposite*, with its marble Venus, serape rug, brocade-strung botanical prints, and worldly mix of antiques, is a visitor's introduction to this house of uncommon character.

■ **In the foyer, a beguiling blend of antiquities offers a perfect introduction to Laurie Warren's house.**

■ **This stately, tree-shaded Victorian is home for Laurie, her family, and her ever-growing collections.**

*The Connecticut home of Laurie Adams Warren is a joyful testimony to her love of "all things wonderful" and to the yearning for change she will not harness.*

■ **An authentic Victorian gazebo is a lovely adjunct to the elegant 1860s house.**

# ALL THINGS BEAUTIFUL

■

**Laurie acquired this topped-with-bric-a-brac Jacobean chest by trading old pieces of silver.**

**B**ecause variety and change are the spice of her design philosophy, Laurie frequently modifies and rearranges her furnishings and collections to create fresh new looks. Nothing stays the same for long. So change-oriented is Laurie that she has been known to sell (or store) almost the entire contents of her house in order to accommodate new acquisitions. "I know that most people are reluctant to go that far in making changes," Laurie says, "but it has been the best way for me to develop and refine my own personal style."

Richly textured in a medley of tapestry, needlepoint, petit point, and white-on-white embroidery, the living room is but one expression of Laurie's ever-evolving eclectic style.

In the family room,
Laurie made use of a
colorful strié fabric to
meld a mixed bag of
furnishings. Used as
slipcovers on the sofa
and chairs, then
repeated again at the
picture window, the
fabric imbues the
white-painted, beamed-
ceiling room with a
cozy country French
feeling.

**D**espite the variety of periods and styles juxtaposed throughout the house, there's no lack of design cohesion. The family room, *left*, is furnished primarily in country French, but the admix extends to England. The sofa, a long-ago gift from Laurie's mother, has been re-covered on numerous scene-changing occasions, as have the two wing chairs. A trio of English Staffordshire dogs and an old wooden child's horse have survived a variety of design transitions; so have the go-anywhere Oriental rugs.

Connected to the family room is an informal dining area used by the Warrens on everyday occasions. The view *at right* shows a small slice of the old Biedermeier dining table, and a full view of a charming corner vignette, featuring an old scrubbed pine chest topped with crystal and books, and an artful arrangement of paintings.

■
**Shedding light on this charming scene is an English Staffordshire dog wired as a lamp.**

aurie is a believer that style is something you develop over a period of time. "It takes trial and error, fits and starts, before you can develop a true sense of who you are and what you really like," says Laurie, adding, "I went through several periods of loving one thing, then realizing later that it wasn't for me."

Laurie's interest in collecting began in the early days of her marriage, when her husband was stationed overseas. As a way to pass the time, she started attending auctions and poking around flea markets. Thus, what started as a pastime, developed into a passion, and—of late—into a profitable business.

Several years ago, Laurie and a similarly "afflicted" friend decided to channel their interests and talents by opening an antiques shop. Here they not only sell things from their own burgeoning collections, but seek new acquisitions for their clients. Says Laurie, "The business has provided a tremendous outlet for me. After all, one can't just keep on collecting ad infinitum."

■ In Laurie's house, even the smallest nooks and corners are styled with exacting detail.

■ A pair of antique four-posters adds a regal touch to the softly pretty guest room.

■ The serenely styled master bedroom is furnished with an antique brass-and-iron bed, old lace curtains, and 1930s seating pieces upholstered in gold brocade.

# ALL THINGS BEAUTIFUL

Taking a cue from her New England ancestors, Laurie styled her newly remodeled 20x20-foot kitchen in the vein of an old-fashioned keeping room. But rather than go overboard with an old-world look, Laurie created fascinating contrast by juxtaposing contemporary all-white backgrounds and work surfaces with down-home country antiques. Particularly striking is the way she has snuggled the rustic stools against a high-style, ceramic-topped work counter. Recessed spotlights dramatize the new/old differences.

■

**The kitchen keeping room is designed with an intriguing blend of old and new elements.**

■

**An old painted cupboard stands confident in the face of contemporary contrast.**

*To create a beautiful balance between old and new, interior designer Ruth Tempel Touhill removed the wrinkles—but not the character—from her '20s-era St. Louis condominium.*

■ **Tastefully furnished with antiques and international classics, the Touhill living room has English manners but a worldly personality.**

# BEST OF BOTH WORLDS

It's not that Ruth Tempel Touhill doesn't like old buildings. She does. And it's not that she isn't enamored of antiques. She is. It's just that Ruth, an individualist, is drawn to contemporary, too.

Home for Ruth and her husband, Tom, is the top floor of a St. Louis three-flat, a 60-year-old building that the couple own. After renovating the first two floors of the building, the Touhills remodeled their own living quarters, reshaping spaces in a modern-day mien, but leaving the old fireplace, leaded glass windows, and lovely floors intact.

■ The Touhills bought this stately old building and styled it—architecturally and decoratively—to their liking.

■ A contemporary lamp sheds light on a marble-topped farm table, accessorized with old books and assorted English antiques.

31

# BEST OF BOTH WORLDS

■ This view from the dining room shows the easy connection to the light-filled living room and solarium beyond.

■ Ruth likes her colors neutral and her textures high-touch. Sofas in the living room and solarium are loosely covered, English-style, in soft linens and natural cottons.

In her role as professional interior designer, Ruth advises beginners to stick with classic designs, furnishings that can be counted on to never look dated or faddish. "Be they antique or contemporary, European or American, classic furnishings invariably look good together, and they acclimate easily to all kinds of architectural surroundings," she explains. Ruth's timeless approach to decorating is evident in her own remodeled old/new milieu, where modern classics like Hans Wegner's "Peacock" chair, and Bertoia's sculptured "diamond" chair, *above*, are paired with a traditional down-filled sofa and a contemporary chrome-and-glass coffee table. Tying together the solarium scheme is a highly patterned Tunisian tribal rug placed—with moxie—on top of the original black-and-white marble floor.

■ Something new in the sunroom is a spiral staircase that leads to Ruth's attic-level office.

# BEST OF BOTH WORLDS

■

**A door in Ruth's functionally furnished attic office leads to a yet-to-be-built outdoor balcony, and a pleasing view of St. Louis.**

To get the space they wanted, the Touhills converted three apartments on the top floor of their building to a single, 3,400-square-foot space. Ruth personally supervised the remodeling and devised the plan for raising the sun porch ceiling in order to create an office, *below*, in the previously inaccessible attic.

Ruth also gets credit for redesigning the kitchen, *opposite*, to include a small dining cafe.

■

**In the cafe dining nook, old card table chairs sit well with a contemporary clear-glass table.**

# BEST OF
# BOTH
# WORLDS

Not all of Ruth's old things are antique. In fact, many of her favorite possessions are serendipitous acquisitions from flea markets, Goodwill, and good friends.

The headboard in the master bedroom counts in the "lucky find" category, as do the dressing-table lamps. Ruth purchased the ersatz French provincial headboard (actually two headboards) for $20 from a now-defunct hotel. After stripping away the gilding and removing the tacked-on plastic backrests, Ruth refinished the exposed wood areas and—using a staple gun—re-covered the backrests with men's gray flannel suiting material. Adding to the bed's beauty is a "new" spread that's actually an antique linen tablecloth embroidered with cutwork. The pillowcases, too, are antique.

The charming dressing table, with its Goodwill lamps, bamboo Regency mirror, and cluster of antique silver frames, is an old library table covered with a skirt made of sheets. Oddly enough, the only new item in this wonderfully nostalgic vignette is the antique-looking Flemish petit-point and needlepoint chair.

■
**The highlight of the room is a new reproduction of an antique petit-point chair.**

■ The prettiest room in
the Touhills' house is
the master bedroom,
where antiques and
fortuitous secondhand
finds commingle.

# FAUX FINESSE

Jon Hattaway and Martin Potter are professional painters, but not the conventional kind. Their forte is faux—a fool-the-eye painting technique that makes plain surfaces look like something they're not: marble, malachite, metal, or wood grains, for example. The partners' work ranges from what they call

■ **Faux is flattering—especially when bargains are beautified with painted finishes.**

"architectural painting" in private homes to a full line of faux-finished accessories that are sold in specialty shops.

Jon's and Martin's keen design sense is wonderfully evident in their own residence, a Victorian duplex in Boston. Imaginatively furnished with antiques, "eccentricities," and numerous examples of their faux creations, the apartment brims with originality and mind-over-money surprises. "It's like playing a game to see how much we can do for the least cost," says Jon, adding, "The trick is to start with a

few good pieces and embellish from there."

The Hattaway/Potter living room boasts a variety of high-dash, low-cash ideas. Amid an eclectic mix of Victorian, Empire, and flea-market furnishings are faux-finished tables, slipcovers made from artist's canvas, and clever window treatments featuring lengths of polished cotton looped and knotted over faux-painted bamboo poles. Also in evidence is a large collection of Napoleonana, including a variety of prints depicting the emperor in his many guises.

*The inimitable decorating style of business partners Jon Hattaway and Martin Potter is everywhere evident in their character-filled Boston duplex apartment.*

■ **Afternoon delight: sun shining on a papier-maché painted table and two Sheraton spider-back chairs.**

■ **An English hussar on a horse cavorts across an antique Empire chest.**

# FAUX FINESSE

Upstairs, the mood of the duplex subtly shifts, becoming warmer, cozier, and more informal. But though the ambience is different, design ideas continue to abound.

The dining room, with three views pictured here, is especially pleasing. One clever touch is the way an antique, rope-turned drop-leaf table has been teamed, out of context, with primitive, rush-seated chairs and a matching settee, all from Haiti. "Sometimes, customers order this Haitian furniture painted in faux finishes, but for a change of pace, we left ours untouched," explains Jon.

Adding to the contrast of rustic and refined are the antique linen dish towels that are draped gracefully and unexpectedly on chairbacks to serve as dinner napkins.

Other inspiring ideas: an old footbath used as a flower container on the painted chest, *opposite;* a soufflé dish turned into a flowery center-piece; and an antique rug and framed Victorian crazy quilts hung on the wall as artwork.

■ Placed against a brick wall, a 19th-century scrubbed-pine linen press makes a beautiful stowaway for dining room paraphernalia.

■ The hand-painted *faux bois* fireplace wall is a fine example of Hattaway's and Potter's talents.

■ A 19th-century grain-painted chest is the pièce de résistance in the dining room.

# FAUX
# FINESSE

There's something about the guest room/sitting room/den that calls to mind a cozy Parisian pied-à-terre. The faux-painted rosewood daybeds, covered in paisley and piled high with a colorful mélange of chintz-covered pillows, are definitely French in feeling. So are the walls, painted a Dijon mustard color, and the arrangement of Napoleonic posters and prints, all displayed in Hattaway/Potter faux-painted frames.

■ Nestled next to the red leather chair is an inexpensive parsons table, artfully updated with a stylized tortoiseshell finish.

■ Designed with continental flair, the combination guest room/sitting room is pleasantly crowded with color, pattern, and personality.

Wit, whimsy, ingenuity, and charm—these are the ingredients used here, and throughout Hattaway's and Potter's highly personal house.

43

# THE RITCHKEN RESIDENCE

**D**eborah and Simon Ritchken have always been intrigued with interior design, architecture, and art. On their first date they went to an art festival, and they've enjoyed gallery hopping ever since. But there's irony in this story. "As our tastes have become more sophisticated and refined, they've also become more expensive. The problem with being 'into' design is that you end up not liking anything or you no longer can afford what you like. One runs the risk of becoming an immobilized aesthete," observes Deborah.

To solve this conundrum, the Ritchkens have taken a minimalist design approach. "We don't buy much, and we don't buy often, but when we do, it's usually one really great thing."

*Following the old caveat "Take your time," Deborah and Simon Ritchken have turned their recently remodeled house into a less-is-more modern retreat.*

■ The "one really great thing" in front of the fireplace is a pair of Josef Hoffmann-style "graffiti" chairs.

■ Styled like a gallery, the two-level living room features '20s-era seating pieces covered in gray silk.

45

Many of the Ritchkens' furnishings, including the table and chairs in the skylighted dining room, were designed by architect John Nalevanko, the same man who remodeled parts of their house.

■ A built-in wall of cubicles showcases the Ritchkens' ceramics collection.

■ Perched on a stairwell in the kitchen dining area, a hand-carved bird has its beak directed toward an errant apple.

The Ritchkens are interested in all kinds of art, but their passion is ceramics. "We bought our first piece on our first date and we are still at it," says Deborah. A built-in display wall, *above*, dramatizes their treasured, one-of-a-kind collection, and also serves to separate the open-plan dining area from the kitchen. At any given time, there are always empty display cubicles because the Ritchkens like to feature individual pieces by rotating them to other parts of the house. One such ceramic is now "on loan" to the dining room, *opposite*, where it serves as a sculptural centerpiece.

# THE
# RITCHKEN
# RESIDENCE

Although it's minimalist in terms of the *amount* of furnishings, the atmosphere of the Ritchkens' house is far from monastic. Take the bedroom, for example. The Memphis-style bed and the just-for-a-spoof "suburban" chair (with a white picket fence serving as a backrest and a seat styled like a kidney-shape pool) are spirited, not Spartan, in character. Lest you think that furniture-as-art isn't functional, the pyramid-shape headboard houses all of the necessities normally found on a conventional nightstand, and the chair—admittedly not comfortable—can be sat on.

Adjoining the master bedroom is a new his-and-hers bathroom designed by architect Nalevanko to pamper the Ritchkens with spalike luxury.

■
**The sculptural beauty of the imported twin basins is redoubled by a mirrored background.**

■
**Angled to face a view-worthy picture window, the furniture-as-art pyramid bed has a funky Memphis-style flavor.**

# *GETTING PERSONAL*

*What another would have done*

*as well as you, do not do it....*

*Be faithful to that which exists*

*nowhere but in yourself.*

André Paul Guillaume Gide, *Les Nourritures Terrestres, Envoi*

# PRIZED COLLECTIONS

███████ *Getting personal involves nothing more and nothing less than putting yourself in the picture. It means giving an eviction notice to all things anonymous and inconsequential, then focusing on the things that you—and your family—really love. It doesn't matter whether the objects of your affection are simple or splendorous, homespun or high style. What does matter is that they mean a lot to you.*

■
**Providing this room with personal distinction is a fine collection of antique American pewter, amassed over a period of years.**

A foyer is an excellent place to announce your passion for a particular thing. Here a collection of old painted boxes and duck decoys greets guests as they come in the door.

Wax elegantly: A sizable collection of old English brass candlesticks, displayed en masse, imbues this dining room side table with distinction.

To give star status to a treasured collection of 19th-century Staffordshire and Leeds china, this dining room cupboard was painted a theatrical shade of coral red.

# FOND MEMORIES

Never hesitate to celebrate *yourself with a display of cherished mementos. Photographs, souvenirs, and keepsakes are the most vital clues to our lives and our loves, and our surroundings are vitalized by their presence.*

■ **This delightful display of childhood valentines is near and dear to the owner's heart.**

■ **Part of the fun of displaying photographs is selecting the frames in which to put them.**

■ **A mantel is a perfect place to make your mark with a grouping of old family photos.**

# CHERISHED HEIRLOOMS

*Although heirlooms are by definition old and honorable, they needn't be regarded as relics. Indeed, you and your environment will be greatly enriched if you incorporate references to the past in your present-day life. And remember, it isn't necessary to give prominence to all of your heirlooms. The idea is to select the items that have special appeal, then use them in your own individual way.*

■
**In this white-walled domain, contemporary instincts are mellowed by the presence of an antique quilt.**

■ **Joys in the attic:** This embroidered pillow sham was rescued from a forgotten trunk to become the focus of a nostalgic scheme.

■ **Inherited genius:** Pay no heed if your house is contemporary and your heirloom furnishings are not. Modern architecture is open-minded and doesn't notice age differences. Proof is this dining room, with its rococo chairs and stark, angular walls.

■ The star of this memory-laden scene is a rough-grained, hand-carved bed from Portugal. Topped with the downiest of pillows and the finest Chinese cotton linens, the antique bed is a family treasure that is treated, not as a hands-off relic, but as a fully functioning piece of furniture.

# TEMPTING TABLETOPS

*When thoughtfully propped with life's little pleasures, a table becomes a personal gallery to be seen and savored by others. Though compositions can consist of just about anything, your tablescape will be most intriguing if it includes at least one surprise.*

■ The surprise element in this still life is a nonconformist lamp.

■ Here three tabletop faithfuls—fruit, flowers, and books—are given new sparkle by the presence of glittering glass.

■ Sitting solo on a circular table, a marble ball grabs the attention of all who walk by.

■ Placed in concert, a mélange of treasures forms a cohesive whole.

Home rule: Even the
most casually
appointed dining room
is fit for a queen.

# WIT AND WHIMSY

*There's nothing like a bit of levity to relax an uptight, too-studied room. Indeed, humor in decoration—visual puns, whimsical artwork, fanciful accessories, or subtle spoofs— is the best palliative for straitlaced surroundings, and can always be counted on to invest a room with personal qualities.*

■ **Horseplay: Though it's serious sculpture, this life-size wire equine has amusing artistic appeal.**

■ **A show of hands— and beaded handbags— are just-for-jest accessories in this tabletop vignette.**

# WIT AND WHIMSY

■
**Split personality:
Designed by folk artist
Bill Jauquet, this two-
section, hand-carved
bust never fails to
pique curiosity and
prompt smiles. Keeping
company with the bust
are an antique
checkerboard and an
old wooden measure.**

Grin and bear it:
Propped on a fireplace
mantel, a beguiling
collection of personable
teddies adds greatly to
the charm of this room.

# SPECIAL FINDS

*Whether your travels take you to faraway places or on meanderings close to home, always keep your feelers out for special, seldom-met finds. Often, it is those fluky acquisitions—collectibles, indescribables, and just-for-fun trifles— that free our homes from the shackles of sameness and fill our hearts with delight.*

■ Anything that fascinates you is fodder for personal style. Here it's plain to see that the owner's passions run to folk art.

■
Your pride-and-joy possessions deserve spectacular display. Here a something-special three-masted ship model has been placed triumphantly on a window ledge to share top billing with the Boston skyline.

■
Public spirit: This copper New York City Fire Department extinguisher-turned-lamp, rich with the patina of age, has adapted beautifully to homey surroundings.

# TINY TREASURES

*The "scenes" you create with tiny treasures can be just as arresting as a work of art. For best results, think of your table as an empty canvas on which interesting shapes, colors, and textures will be applied. Place low objects toward the front of your "picture," and tall ones toward the rear. Then, once you're satisfied with your still life, "frame" it with a lamp, a vase of flowers, or a plant.*

■ Hop to it: Pint-size porcelain rabbits are winsome choices for tabletop displays.

■ Placed on a window ledge, Noah's Ark—and a full complement of painted, hand-carved animals—is a pleasure to behold.

Arranged with the precision of a practiced eye, this elegant assemblage of personal accessories invites the viewer to reach out and touch.

# ARRANGING FOR ART

*The learned understand the reason of art; the unlearned feel the pleasure.*

Quintilian

# INSTANT IMPACT

*Take a quick look at the three living rooms pictured here, then imagine them minus their artwork. Nice, maybe, but knockouts, no. What sets these rooms apart from the crowd is the use of bold, high-impact art. The paintings are more than a passive presence—they're the major design elements that give each room its distinctive decorative character.*

■ In this small living room, art appears, not as an afterthought, but as an integral part of the subtly elegant decorating scheme.

■ Another way to achieve instant impact with art is to hang a series of paintings or prints in close proximity.

■ Here a single powerful painting, flanked by a pair of sculptured Noguchi paper lanterns, creates a dramatic focal point.

# ALL OF A KIND

■ To give added
prominence to this
quartet of hunt prints,
they were matted in
wide bands of white.

*Fine-art prints—especially those depicting a single theme—are excellent wall enhancers. Most collections look their best when identically framed and displayed in close-knit groupings. If scattered about the room, prints tend to lose their decorative potency.*

■ Here a red-painted wall
brings out the beauty
of a framed collection
of botanical prints.

■ Tongue-in-chick: A
tiered arrangement of
rooster prints adds a
whimsical touch to this
entryway.

Bathed in bold artwork
and bright colors, this
under-the-eaves
bathroom is something
special.

80

# WHERE
# YOU WANT IT

■
**This colorful poster
of a potbellied clown
reminds the cook to
watch his diet.**

*People who are stingy with
artwork—who limit its presence to just a
few rooms or a few walls in the house—
are doing themselves (and their decors) a
disservice. Indeed, since it is art's purpose
to please the eye and personalize the
surroundings, there is no place where art
shouldn't be. Are you using art to its
utmost in your house?*

■
**Art can go anywhere:
Here a summer porch is
home to a wonderful
painting, casually
propped on an offbeat
three-legged bench.**

# SIMPLE STATEMENTS

*The "less is more" look is an elegant one that embraces simplicity and eschews the superfluous. Art's role in understated schemes is to make a strong aesthetic statement, but in a subtle, soothing way. Pictured here are two minimalist decorating schemes where art commands attention in an unassuming way.*

■
**A pair of antique Korean calligraphy panels provides Oriental counterpoint for this contemporary setting.**

■
**Art is very much a part of this high-style scheme, but the message is exquisitely subtle.**

# FURNITURE AS ART

███████ *Many of the world's most famous architects and artists are or were talented furniture designers as well. Thanks to the likes of Le Corbusier, Eero Saarinen, Marcel Breuer, and others, we are able to furnish our homes, not just with function, but with mesmerizing shapes that stand alone as art forms.*

■
**Sculpture to sit on: Gerrit Rietveld's evocative Z chair zaps this setting with incisive geometry.**

■
**Don't be modest: If you own something as shapely as Le Corbusier's classic chaise, by all means show it off.**

# BREAKING THE MOLD

*If a man does not keep pace with his
companions, perhaps it is because he
hears a different drummer. Let
him step to the music which he hears,
however measured or far away....*

————————————————

Henry David Thoreau

# STYLE: FOLLOW YOUR INSTINCTS

*In the realm of interior design, it's quite possible to be a nonconformist without being wildly eccentric or weirdly avant garde. The trick is to turn your thinking cap in a different direction, to be accepting of new ideas, and—most of all—to allow the unique voice within you to speak out.*

■
This bungalow is the home of an Anglophile whose tastes are fun-loving and fickle. The English leanings are evidenced by the floral chintz and the very British, fringed lampshade. What's not expected, but certainly welcome, is the colorful contemporary artwork and assorted just-for-a-lark accessories.

# STYLE: STEER CLEAR OF CLICHÉS

■ Here's another example of what good things can happen when stereotypes are banned from the scene. Stripped of curios, curtains, quilts, and the like, this bedroom shines in a sea of whiteness, simply embellished, but not austere.

■ Too much of a good thing can produce unwanted results. A room overloaded with prosaic examples of a "look" runs the risk of looking trite. This cozy sitting room, though country in flavor, is refreshingly free of corny clichés. It's the furnishings—not the furbelows—that make the essential point.

# STYLE: SUITE TO PLEASE

■ From the purple-painted bookshelves to the tables and chests casually draped with old shawls and oddments of fabric, this cozy attic bedroom speaks beautifully of the bibliophile who lives here.

■ A minuscule hideaway, complete with built-in secretary and European-style window shutters, adds to the personal character of this bedroom under the eaves *at left.*

# STYLE:
# AS YOU LIKE IT

■ The mood of this dining room is affected by the presence—or absence—of slipcovers. When company comes, the chrome-and-cane chairs are dressed in cotton; the rest of the time they're counterpoints for the antique table.

■ Mind over money: It took clever ideas, not a big bankbook, to create this relaxed summer-house scheme. The sofas are home-made, as are the boxes-as-bookshelves and the hand-painted mantel. The real conversation piece, however, is the see-through acrylic coffee table supported by a brigade of painted plastic soldiers.

# STYLE: COMBINE CULTURES

■ Just as ethnic foods add spice to our tables, worldly goods add oomph to our rooms. Here cultural charisma is provided by a colorful collection of American Indian rugs.

■ Open-door policy: Though it's located in the desert Southwest, this adobe interior has been deftly furnished with foreign relations, namely four French chairs, a Mexican rug, and floor pillows covered in south-of-the-border horse blankets.

# COLOR:
# TRY A NEW HUE

*It takes pluck to stray from the safety of a noncommittal color scheme, but gumption is a must if you want to wake up a decoratively do-nothing room. To muster your courage, remember this saying: "You can't make an omelet without first breaking eggs."*

■
You'll strike it rich—stylewise—if you paint your walls a refreshingly irreverent color. Here raspberry was used as a relaxing influence in this formally furnished sitting room.

■
Instant ambience: Deep sapphire blue walls wrap this library/living room in a cocoon of intimacy and warmth. Punctuated with white, the dark, moody color provides a striking backdrop for furnishings, artwork, and accessories.

■ Strokes of brilliance: This living room's winning color combination—peach, white, and periwinkle blue—was plucked from the dhurrie rug that defines the fireside seating area.

# COLOR: PICK A PASTEL

■ The pastels of the past—pallid, barely-there colors—have been replaced with deliciously tempting tints. Particularly popular are watercolor hues that wash a room with impressionistic light. This small sitting room is colored softly in a soothing palette of seafoam green.

# COLOR: CALL ON CHROMAS

■

Chromas are the extroverts of the color spectrum—their outgoing personalities are guaranteed to gladden the spirits while bringing visual excitement to any room in the house. Here, a jolt of bright yellow keeps this formally furnished town house from looking too straitlaced.

■

Here's eye-catching proof that purple and red needn't be strange bedfellows. The combination, though daring, is a stylish alternative to a typical somnolent scheme.

# COLOR: BRAVE THE ELEMENTS

■

If contemporary style is your preference, you'll be captivated by the new geologics. These are colors that simulate the look of earthy elements such as slate, marble, alabaster, granite, and various metals. Here, a pair of classic chairs have been slipcovered in shiny faux metal fabric.

■

Geologic colors are great pretenders. Hand-cut "stones" of rice paper, a travertine desk top, and a gunmetal chintz bedspread combine to give an ordinary attic bedroom the look of new-age antiquity.

# FURNITURE: RELAX THE RULES

*It used to be that a room wasn't "right" unless it decoratively conformed to the "rules." The eclectic look was the eccentric look, a peculiar style to be shunned. But happily, times have changed. Prescribed surroundings are a thing of the past, and the matched look is déclassé. Whenever you can, ignore convention in favor of upbeat élan.*

■
The allure of this aerie apartment lies in its assured, but unstudied, look. Disparate pieces—including an Empire-style Duncan Phyfe sofa, a linen-covered Salvation Army chair, a betasseled moiré slipper chair, an art deco chest, and a bold floral area rug—have been assembled assertively with enviable results.

107

# FURNITURE: OUT OF CONTEXT

■ If you're fond of furnishings that don't fit the mold, worry not. Often, it's the most curious combinations that do the most to delight. Here, black-lacquered bank chairs and pink-cushioned porch furniture seem wonderfully right for this city setting.

■ It's not just okay—it's au courant—to bring a chaise longue in from the cold. This chaise, formerly a British campaign bed, spends its summers on a screened-in porch.

109

# FURNITURE: MIX OLD AND NEW

■

Don't close the door on a piece of furniture just because it's much newer or older than the things you already have. Here, an upstart turquoise table makes easy friends when placed in company with traditional furnishings.

■

A medley of old wicker, modern Memphis, lipstick-red leather, and shiny tubular metal works magic in this up-in-the-treetops contemporary setting.

111

# FURNITURE: SEEK THE UNIQUE

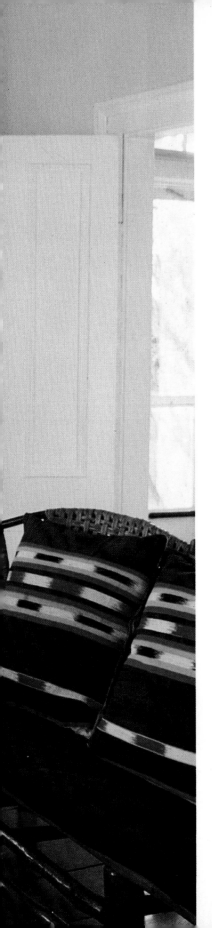

■ Nature provides: This ordinary dinette table was turned into a treasure by wrapping the chrome pedestal base with dried sunflower stalks. The unusual wallpaper? It's a homemade decoupage of brown wrapping paper laminated with torn pieces of white kraft paper.

■ This sitting room owes its singular charm to an exciting amalgam of elements. The rough-hewn settee and chairs are 19th-century adirondack pieces, the tables are Victorian, the horse prints are English, and the colorful cushions were made from the sling of a modern-day Mexican hammock. More panache is provided by a zingy Oriental rug and a madly ornate Italian lamp base.

113

# ARRANGEMENTS: DARE TO BE DIFFERENT

*Arrangement is an aspect of personal style that often gets overlooked. This is unfortunate, because a room is bound to suffer in terms of style, comfort, and/or function if the furniture placement is too predictable or otherwise out of whack. If your present decorating scheme falls short of the mark, it could be the arrangement—not the room itself—that's amiss.*

■
**Forget the requisite sofa: Treat yourself— and your fireplace—to a tête-à-tête grouping of lounge chairs like these. And for put-your-feet-up comfort, be sure to include an ottoman.**

# ARRANGEMENTS: TRY A NEW ANGLE

■ Turn the tables: When space refuses to cooperate with the furnishings on hand, your best bet is to try a new tack. Here an expansive pine table was placed on an angle in order to fit the confines of a narrow, asymmetrical room.

■ If flexibility is your top priority, put modular furnishings on your "must" list. Modulars can be moved with the greatest of ease to suit even the most difficult floor plan. In this living room, a pair of armless chairs were placed on the diagonal to create a buffer for the entryway just behind. A space-efficient L-shape grouping completes the versatile arrangement.

# ARRANGEMENTS: OFFBEAT IDEAS

■ Predictability is the scourge of personal style. If your notions run contrary to the norm, so much the better. In this narrow San Francisco town house, a space-eating sofa was eliminated in favor of four (three are shown) luxurious, leather-covered armchairs.

■ Here's yet another way to buck the obligatory fireside seating arrangement. In lieu of face-to-face sofas, a quartet of quilted slipper chairs form a casual—and convivial— arrangement.

# ARRANGEMENTS: FOOL THE FLOOR PLAN

■ Although the blueprint dubbed it a living room, this cozy space is used variously as a sitting room, dining room, and library/den. Furnishings, including a hefty pedestal table and a pair of English Regency chairs covered in pink pigskin, adapt beautifully to a variety of functions.

■ The disappearing dining room: Except when company comes, this "dining room" doesn't exist. Most of the time, the black-lacquered drop-leaf table is placed against a wall and flanked with the handsome wing chairs. Consider double-duty furnishings like these if you want to avoid the space waste of a one-function room.

# SCHEMING TO PLEASE

*Imagination is the eye of the soul....*

───────────────────────

Joubert

# THE TRADITIONALIST

*Scheming to please involves creating an environment that makes you feel at home. What good, after all, is a picture-perfect room if it fails to accept you for who you are? Whatever your preference in furnishings styles, aim to create a balance between looks and livability. The more closely you relate your decor to your way of life, the happier you—and your family—are bound to be.*

■

**Although the architecture is imposing and the appointments elegant, this living room is a real people-pleaser. Furnishings, including sit-back-and-relax seating pieces, a piano, lots of books, and a chess table set for a game, encourage family gatherings in a warm and friendly way.**

125

■ In a world filled with passing fancies, it's nice to know that some things never go out of style. Traditional designs like these, *left,* can always be counted on to retain their easy-to-live-with appeal.

■ There is something in the genteel nature of a traditional dining room that fosters good manners, promotes conversation, and invites us to linger long after the meal is over. This one, furnished formally with Sheraton and Queen Anne pieces, does just that.

■ True traditionalists are invariably happiest when surrounded by comforting symbols of the past. And what could be more comforting—or comfortable—than a time-honored tester bed. This one is handsomely draped in green-and-beige country French toile.

127

# THE COUNTRY BUFF

■

For many aficionados, collecting things country is an enjoyable hobby that translates into a delightful decorative look. This living room is but one example of what nice things can happen when fortuitous finds are put to imaginative —and practical— interior use.

■

When country speaks with a British accent, the statement is casually elegant. Here, plump, down-filled seating pieces keep company with assorted English antiques and a magnificent collection of blue Imari ware. Dark-stained ceiling beams add to the cozy country-house feeling.

# THE ROMANTIC

■ A little romance—in the form of billowy balloon shades, a come-hither chaise, and vases of just-picked flowers— adds a soft touch to this sophisticated, stripped-down scheme. Other easeful influences include a luxurious mohair throw and several hand-painted silk pillows.

■ Don't skimp on chintz— not if you want to set the stage for a romantic scheme like this one. Yards and yards of the floral fabric swathe the setting in garden colors, calling to mind a storybook cottage on a lovely summer day.

131

# THE MODERNIST

■
This living room
eschews the stark side
of contemporary for a
softer, more sociable
look. The furnishings,
with their shapely
silhouettes, have a
come-hither quality,
and the color scheme is
up-to-the-minute
mellow. A built-in
banquette embraces the
room, adding to its
make-yourself-
comfortable appeal.

*Scheming to Please*
# THE MODERNIST

■ California schemin':
You needn't live on the
Pacific coast to create
a sun-bleached casual
look. Simply do as
these homeowners did
and strip your floors to
their natural state,
raise the ceiling to let
in the light, then—for a
tropical touch—paint
all wall and ceiling
surfaces the palest
shade of banana
yellow. Seating pieces
here are all classic
designs that have been
covered, cabana-style,
in solid pastels and
broad-stripe fabrics.

# THE MIXER

■ The broader your tastes, the more likely you are to embrace an eclectic approach to design. Here, period pieces are masterly paralleled with modern artwork and shapely, contemporary tub chairs dressed for dinner in white.

■ When mixing furniture from different periods and places, always seek a common thread that will tie the disparate elements together. In this living room, unity is provided by color and an emphasis on casual comfort.

■

Texture assumes a leading role in this no-frills neutral scheme. In lieu of color and ornamentation, it's the subtle interplay of tactile surfaces that imbues the room with vitality. Furnishings—including a modular sofa covered in canvas, a soft leather Eames chair, and a rustic trunk-turned-coffee-table—are counter-posed with rough brick walls and red clay floor tiles topped with a nubby area rug.

■

You don't have to be a die-hard traditionalist to incorporate formal furniture into your home. Here a pair of 18th-century French chairs have been rendered comfortable and care free by covering them in channel-quilted cotton duck. Far from looking out of place in this low-key casual setting, the dignified seating pieces are eminently at ease.

# THE SENTIMENTALIST

■

More than anything
else, the sentimentalist
seeks a haven to come
home to—a place where
furnishings are
venerable, comfort is
palpable, and the
surroundings are
etched with smile lines.
Such a place is the
inviting home of two
German-born artists.
Their living room,
furnished with
heirlooms from the
homeland, embraces
the couple beautifully
with comforting
connections to the past.

■ Old-fashioned flair extends to the seating group pictured here. To companionably meld the mix of furnishings, she covered the settee, the wing chair, and the open-arm chair in the same black shell print fabric. Gilt-framed oil paintings and an elegant English gateleg table further the nostalgic feeling.

■ Not one to be influenced by fads, this homeowner prefers to decorate in a purely old-world way. Her living room, with its original beamed ceiling, benefits beautifully from a sentimental approach. Here, cherished antiques commingle amicably with thrift shop finds, lace curtains, candlestick sconces, and timeworn Oriental rugs.

# THE DREAMER

■

A bedroom is a place to indulge your fancies, whatever they may be. Strive to surround yourself with your own brand of comfort, the kind that will refresh your body and revitalize your soul. For the person who lives here, comfort comes from a magnificent brass bed covered luxuriously with Egyptian cotton linens. Serenity is provided by the soothing color scheme and the warmth of the setting sun.

# THE
# DREAMER

■

Coordinated design
collections offer an
almost foolproof way to
add class and dash to a
bedroom. Proof can be
seen in this pattern-
sure setting that's
lavished with linens,
wall coverings, and
fabrics from a stylish
prematched collection.

■

This large master
bedroom is part of a
new addition to a
centuries-old house. In
keeping with the
original architecture,
pine tongue-and-groove
paneling was

incorporated into the
decor, as was a fire-
place. Other amenities
in this restful retreat
include ceiling-reaching
bookshelves, and doors
leading to an idyllic
wicker-furnished porch.

■

For many people, the best part of sleeping is waking up to the sounds and sights of chirping birds, whispering breezes, and dappled sunlight dancing on the walls. If this is your sleep style—and if privacy factors permit—do as these nature-loving homeowners did and leave your bedroom windows totally, temptingly bare. If you *must* cover your windows, pick a barely-there treatment such as sheers, slatted shutters, or translucent shades.

149

# THE CONVIVIAL COOK

■ Designed by and for a gregarious cook, this recently remodeled eat-in kitchen was styled with socializing in mind. Indeed, the new glass-walled dining area is so inviting that it has become the main gathering spot in the house.

■ A combination kitchen/ family room like this one serves up the best of all worlds. In its dual role, the no-wall environment feeds our craving for function and efficiency while providing plenty of sustenance for the soul.

■ This kitchen looks as good as it cooks. The best of tradition (brass hardware, wood trim) lives with elegant modern materials (sandblasted glass doors, stony laminate counters), warmed by rich color from creamy walls and a ruglike mosaic floor. Kitchen kibitzers prop themselves on sinuously shaped stools.

■ In the same kitchen pictured *opposite* is a charming bistro-style dining alcove, *right.* The scene-setting ingredients include painted wicker chairs, open glass shelves, an art nouveau lamp, and a *très* French marquetry-framed mirror.

# THE DINER

The most appetizing dining rooms put forth a promise that pleasures—culinary and companionable—await. This one, formally furnished in period perfection, beckons the diner with an ambrosial ambience of luscious color and flattering light. The tablescape, consisting of fresh flowers, green apples, and individual freesia-filled vases, is (at least partially) good enough to eat.

There's no question that black is a brazen color to use in a dining room, but brazen is the key to this brinkmanship scheme. Just as commanding as the color scheme is the majestic mirror-fronted armoire, placed with authority at the head of the table. Other intrepid influences are the checkerboard floor, the black bentwood chairs, and the wainscoting—actually old doors from a university that the owners salvaged, sawed in half, and installed on the walls.

155

# THE DINER

■

Urbane and elegantly unorthodox, this dining room is a triumph of self-assured style. The recipe: a black circle of solid resin ensphered by a custom-built, faux-finished daybed and a pair of graceful Biedermeier chairs.

■

It's a dining room, yes, hospitably furnished with an antique table and Pennsylvania farmhouse chairs. But more than a pleasant place to eat, this room invites diners to sit a spell—to spend time with a book, to contemplate the art photos propped on a ledge, or to engage in a round-table discussion.

# THE MOPPET

■ Shipboard-style efficiency transformed this shoebox of a room into a charming and functional child's retreat. The "berth" is a custom-built platform bed with a storage drawer beneath. A plastic laminate ledge spans the end of the room, creating a work surface and a slim headboard. At the foot of the bed, a pair of chests provide ample stowing space while adding only inches to the bed's length.

■ The little girl who lives here was treated, by her mother, to a delightful yesteryear look. The cabbage-rose wallpaper, though new, is reminiscent of an earlier era, and befits the graceful beauty of the old-fashioned sleigh bed. Both the bed and the quilt that tops it once belonged to the homeowner's mother, so this room is imbued with sentimental value as well as childlike appeal.

# THE
# MOPPET

■

Personal style—the pint-size variety—is delightful and disarming. The only problem is when budding artists get carried away, using the whole house as their canvas. To encourage creativity and at the same time contain it, consider this solution: a giant-size roll of paper mounted on a floor-to-ceiling bulletin board.

A painted floor is an excellent choice for a child's room. This one, brightly colored in green high-gloss enamel, adds cheer and charm to a playroom setting, and is a snap to keep clean with a broom or a damp mop. Any wood floor—as long as it's stripped of wax or polish, and free of dust—is a candidate for a colorful paint job.

161

This elegant, dark-paneled, English-style library is the kind of room that bibliophiles dream of. Walls and walls of book-lined shelves, plenty of good reading lights, spacious tabletops, and ultra-comfortable seating pieces—these are the things that constitute a booklover's idea of heaven on earth.

162

# THE BOOKWORM

■ If your leanings are literary, you owe it to yourself to find a home for your tomes. The best of all worlds is an entire room reserved for reading material, but if space doesn't allow such luxury, any shelf-lined nook or niche will do. In this cozily furnished library/den, a single wall of built-in shelves serves a family of avid readers well.

# THE BILL PAYER

■ A desk can be a decorative asset in the living room as well as a handy place for paying bills. Here a bay window area was put to work with a desk fashioned from a slab of oak-trimmed laminate supported by a two-drawer file cabinet and a red-painted cement form. The storage unit is a space-saving built-in.

■ The simple strategy of converting two catchall closets into a single wall of shelves and storage cabinets transformed this 12x16-foot room into a handsome home office/ den. Placed between the windows is a spacious "partners" desk that doubles, when needed, as a dining table. When the workday is over, the office does a quick change and becomes a comfortable spot for relaxing, reading, and watching TV. Where's the TV? It's hidden behind closed doors.

This luxurious, newly remodeled bath offers all the amenities an unabashed Sybarite could want. From the silvery tiles to the black mirrored shower door and crystal chandelier, the room glitters with glamour and beckons the bather to indulge. A whirlpool tub invites long, leisurely soaks, and an elegant chaise provides a place to repose while sipping tea and watching the morning news.

# THE BATHER

■ A bathroom needn't be brand-new to be a standout. This bathing beauty, located in a 225-year-old house, is charming because of—not in spite of—its age. Fitted with a French bathtub and a marble sink—both prized acquisitions from a Parisian hotel—the 12x12-foot room features original tongue-and-groove wainscoting and a white-painted, wide-plank floor.

167

# THE RELAXER

■ A site for sore feet: Placed in a solarium, this classic Alvar Aalto chaise is the perfect spot for enjoying sunlit solitude, a short siesta, or a stare into space.

■ There's nothing like an easy chair to make you feel at home. Here, plop-down comfort is provided by a pair of ocean-liner-era armchairs, upholstered to cushy perfection, and a requisite put-your-feet-up ottoman.

# TRY
# SOMETHING
# SPECIAL

*No one knows what he can do till he tries.*

---

Publilius Syrus

# SHOW OFF WITH SHEETS

■ These no-sew slipcovers are made from sheets that are wrapped and pinned in place. Only the cushions are sewn.

■ Two knots are all it took to create this sheet-wrapped cushion.

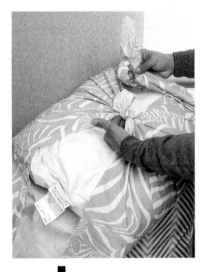

■ More sleight of hand with sheets: To make this handsome room divider, hinge together four artist's stretcher frames, pad the frames, then customize with stapled-on sheets.

*Personal style is yours for the making when you couple your talents with creative decorating techniques. Here and on the following 14 pages, we'll show you a variety of hands-on ideas using sheets, paint, and wallpaper.*

■ If you have decorator taste but a do-it-yourself budget, sheets are an excellent save-money solution. Here, 12 twin-size flat sheets were used to give this bedroom a classy, coordinated look. Four sheets were shirred on rods at the windows, two were turned into no-sew slipcovers, and the rest were fashioned into flounces, a table skirt, and a pretty blanket cover.

■
This detail shows how
the chair and ottoman
cushions are wrapped
package-fashion with
sheet fabric, which is
then secured in place
with T-pins. Note that
the slip-on flounce is
elasticized.

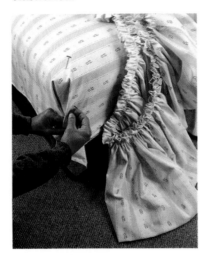

■
The curtains are a
cinch to make. Simply
sew a rod pocket at the
bottom edges of two
twin-size sheets, then
shirr the sheets—and
rod cover—in place.

175

# FAKE IT WITH FAUX

*Faux is one type of fakery you needn't view with disfavor. Quite the contrary. When used to simulate the look of marble and other expensive materials, faux effects can be counted on to invest a plain-Jane room with distinction.*

■ With patience and practice, you can create a magical faux marble finish like this one.

■ Dressing this dining room is a faux marble floor and elegant, painted-on door panels.

■ Faux for the fun of it: This rug is fake, down to the very last fringe.

# PLAY UP WITH PAINT

*When used inventively, paint is more than a cover-up; it's liquid personality. The next time your paintbrush beckons, treat your surroundings to a new technique.*

■ Painted to look like carpet, these stairs are a step up from the ordinary.

■ The walls in this room have been "combed" to produce a tactile, textured finish. To create a similar look, apply a coat of paint, let dry, then apply another coat in a slightly darker color. Before the second coat dries, comb with a ragged-edge implement or a piece of corrugated cardboard.

■ When protected with several coats of polyurethane, a painted floor treatment like this one, *far right*, fends off stains and scuff marks.

178

■ Paint is a great pinch hitter, especially in architecturally featureless rooms. Here, ordinary French doors were elevated to Post-Modern status with a painted-on pediment and a piece of tile.

■ Arch enterprise: In a daring move, this homeowner not only paired modern architecture with mellow antiques, but boldly emphasized the counterpoint with strokes of pink paint.

To add punctuation to this period setting, a small-print wallpaper border was used to create a "frame" for a large oil painting. The same border shows up again to the right of the fireplace as mock architectural molding.

# BEAUTIFY WITH BORDERS

*Small details can make a big difference between a so-so wall treatment and one that's outstanding. Wallpaper borders, in particular, are excellent room enhancers. They come in a wide range of patterns, colors, and design motifs, and look great whether used alone or teamed with coordinated wall coverings.*

■ When used to define and accentuate windows, wallpaper borders are eye-catching alternatives to draperies and curtains. Here a pair of deep-set windows have been framed—in country French fashion—with a winsome floral-and-plaid print.

183

If you're a novice at stenciling, start with a simple design like this one. The leaf motif, inspired by a floral wallpaper pattern, imbues this bathroom's oak floor with color and character.

# STYLE WITH STENCILS

*Look to stencils if you want to give blank walls and bare floors a big dose of distinction. With patience, paint, and sufficient sleight of hand, you can create your own unique stencil designs, or you can use precut stencils from kits.*

■ **This bathroom floor was stripped and bleached before the hand-painted stencil design was applied.**

■ **Stencils are perfect accompaniments for period settings like this charming colonial-style bedroom.**

185

# MAKE BELIEVE WITH MURALS

*Another way to create your own kind of magic is with a hand-painted wall mural. If you're artistically inclined, you'll want to create your own mural design. If you're not, simply adapt a motif from a favorite photo or drawing.*

■ A wave of a muralist's wand transformed this child's room into a fairy-tale fantasyland.

■ This engaging country scene was adapted from an American primitive crewel pattern.

# SPIRITED RENOVATIONS

*We need not power or splendor; wide hall*
*or lordly dome; the good, the true, the tender,*
*these form the wealth of a home.*

————————————————————

Sara J. Hale

The living room retains many old-world features of the original brownstone, including the ornate fireplace and ceiling moldings.

# A LIGHT-FILLED BROWNSTONE

Although it's as long and narrow as a railway car (50x15 feet), this 110-year-old brownstone is deceptively spacious inside. By tearing out a surfeit of interior walls, then adding a 25-foot-high atrium at the rear of the building, architect Stuart M. Narofsky created a light-filled living area that overlooks a lovely patio. The owners of this urban dwelling are delighted with the redo. As former suburbanites, they yearned for a "real" house with a "real" yard, and Narofsky's solution comes as close as possible to providing them with both.

■
**A sculptured glass facade incorporates French doors that open directly to the patio.**

# A LIGHT-FILLED BROWNSTONE

**T**o facilitate alfresco entertaining and to provide an unobstructed view of the walled-in patio and garden, Narofsky placed the newly renovated dining room/kitchen area on ground level, just below the balcony of the second-story living room. Minimal city-slick furnishings, uncluttered backgrounds, recessed lighting, and sleek oak flooring laid on the diagonal all work beautifully to promote the illusion of space in the narrow, 15-foot-wide room.

■

**A tree grows—not in Brooklyn—but in the light-flooded atrium of this once-dreary Manhattan brownstone.**

■

**The contemporary kitchen, though in plain view of the dining area, is an unobtrusive presence.**

# VILLAGE IN A CITY LOFT

**I**t's one thing to envision living in an industrial loft, but another to figure out how to make a former factory feel homey. For architect David Haymes and his partner, George Pappageorge, the solution was uniquely inventive: They domesticated their 2,400 square feet of soaring space by turning it into a fascinating interior "village."

■
**Three multilevel pavilions house the loft's bedrooms, kitchen, and baths.**

■
**David Haymes' delightful indoor village is located in this old Chicago factory.**

# VILLAGE IN A LOFT

**A**rchitect Haymes combined structural know-how with a sense of fun to create his intriguing village-in-a-loft. Looking like a make-believe stage set, the houselike pavilions that surround the main living/dining area are actually enclosures for functional rooms. Referring to the photograph on pages 194–195, the pavilion to the rear of the dining area houses a bathroom on the lower level and a sleeping loft on top. The structure in the middle contains a kitchen below and a sauna above. A second bathroom is located behind the yellow bay window, and there's a small sitting area on the balcony level above.

Completing the village-in-a-loft illusion is the spacious living/dining area that serves as the loft's "town square." It is here, surrounded by 10x10-foot windows, that guests gather to enjoy themselves and to marvel at Haymes' architectural achievement.

■ Located just in front of the bath/bedroom pavilion is a compact home office.

■ A buffet counter connects the kitchen to the open dining area.

■ Furnishings in the loft's
main living area are
just as fun and inven-
tive as the architecture.

197

# AN UPDATED CARRIAGE HOUSE

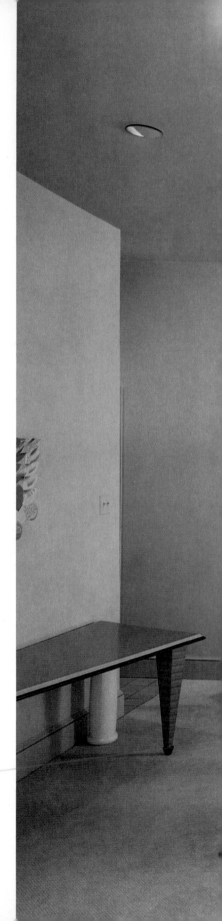

*The staid facade of this 19th-century carriage house belies the contemporary ambience that awaits inside.*

It took a daring rescue effort to turn this 1890s carriage house into a bold showcase of contemporary design. At one time the servants quarters for an elegant St. Louis mansion, the building—now owned by Ginny and Steve Bonne—sat empty for years before it was renovated by architect Don Royse.

The stalwart exterior, with its handsome Federal detailing, offers no clues to the trans-formation inside. In redoing the house, Royse made no attempt to recapture the look of a bygone era. For one thing, there was nothing special to capture. The building, though sporting a grand exterior, was unremarkable inside.

Royse's tack was to create character through contrast. His new open floor plan offers many spatial surprises and provides an exciting milieu for the Bonnes' contemporary artwork and furnishings.

■ **In its former life, the carriage house was used as servants quarters.**

■ **Neon strip lighting offers a bold departure from a traditional dining room chandelier.**

Within a century-old shell, soaring spaces and sleek furnishings fast-forward the hands of time.

The Bonnes' decorating scheme is just as dramatic as the architecture. With the help of interior designer Marcia Smith, they combined contemporary furniture with vivid colors and special lighting effects to create a look that's thoroughly upbeat. Ginny and Steve are avid entertainers, and they use their large, two-story living room, *opposite* and *right,* primarily for large cocktail parties. A small, intimately furnished den is used when "it's just the two of us," explains Ginny.

Rather than chop up the "milling" space with assorted sofas, tables, and chairs, designer Smith emphasized the room's open feeling by limiting seating to a single grouping of easy-to-move-about modular pieces. Arranged in front of the black marble fireplace, the meandering sofa provides plenty of comfortable seating for 10 or more people.

Because the adventurous architecture is an art form in itself, Smith saw no need to gussy up the room with extraneous decoration. All of the wall surfaces (with one exception) are painted stark white. The art deco fireplace, with its striking stair-step design, has been boldly punctuated in blue. The room's only other color comes from leafy plants, graphic-patterned toss pillows, and several other carefully chosen accessories. The walls are free of artwork and the windows are beautifully bare. With no distractions to get in the way, the eye is free to explore and enjoy the soaring spaces.

The view *opposite* provides a glimpse of the balcony sitting area and the redesigned entrance hall below. It is in this foyer, with its modern glass brick walls and quarry tile floor, that guests get their first inkling that this is no ordinary house.

■

**A black marble art-deco-style fireplace is the focal point of the two-story room.**

The second story of the carriage house echoes the exuberant spirit of the first floor. With no venerable woodwork to worry about restoring, architect Royse was free to reshape the upstairs rooms in a totally contemporary vein.

The master bedroom, *opposite,* features a fanciful interplay of geometric shapes. Steel rods, welded into the shape of a cube, form a transparent sanctuary for the bed. Placed at an angle to the walls and windows, the bed—with its "stepped" art deco headboard and bright red spread—becomes an eye-catching art form, not just a place to sleep.

Equally arresting is the adjoining bathroom, *right,* with its gleaming mirrors and glossy ceramic tiles. Repeated reflections by walls of mirror add depth to the room and make it appear larger than it really is. Adding extra dash are the colorful columns used as supports for twin washbasins.

■
**A bold color scheme of coral, red, and black imbues the bedroom with character.**

■
**Materials for the new master bath reflect the fun and vigor of the rest of the house.**

# THE LIBERATED RANCH

It's easy to malign a typical 1950s-style ranch house. Most were built as poky places with rooms the size of cubicles, skimpy windows, low ceilings, and floor plans that were awkward at best. Millions of these prosaic ranches still exist, but some, happily, have been liberated from their mundane pasts.

*Here's beautiful proof that it's possible to rescue a hopelessly dated ranch house from a bad case of the blahs.*

Take this one for example: It used to be as chopped up and cramped as a house can get. But now, thanks to an artful renovation effort that involved removing walls, ripping out carpet, raising the roof, and adding many new windows, the ranch is not only free of 1950s confines, but gloriously attuned —both decoratively and architecturally—to today.

■ **Reviving the living room involved raising the roof, baring the floor, and trading blank walls for windows.**

■ **Passersby are none the wiser that this handsome house is a 1950s ranch in disguise.**

# THE LIBERATED RANCH

**P**erhaps the most annoying thing about 1950s-era houses—be they ranches, bungalows, or basic boxes—is their small, barely functional kitchens. In this house, the original kitchen was tucked, like an afterthought, into a dining room corner; there was nothing personable—and little usable—about it. To give the new owners the cooking-for-pleasure kitchen they wanted, designer Mariette Himes Gomez commandeered the dwelling's unused garage and turned it into the sleek Eurostyle kitchen pictured *below*.

The old shoebox of a kitchen and dining area is now long gone. In its place is this sophisticated dining room, *opposite*, complete with French doors and a skylight.

■ **What used to be a breezeway between kitchen and garage is now an elegant, glassed-in foyer.**

■ **The ranch's pared-down dining room is geared for practical comfort.**

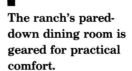

■ **The owners have no regrets about relinquishing their garage for a fabulous new kitchen.**

# A STONE BARN RENEWED

■ **The great-room, with its open loft and vaulted ceiling, is irresistibly inviting.**

■ **Glenfiddich Farm is a haven for white-tailed deer and wild turkeys.**

Janet and Louis LeHane are the very lucky owners of Glenfiddich Farm, a bucolic 19-acre country place, complete with a delightful stone house that once was a barn. Located on the outskirts of Leesburg, Virginia—just a one-hour drive from Washington, D.C.—the 1840s barn was partially converted by the previous owners in 1971, then painstakingly perfected by the LeHanes in 1979.

As you can see, the LeHanes' thoughtful renovation efforts have paid off in beautiful dividends.

*Although effectively restyled for easy living and gracious entertaining, Glenfiddich Farm retains its warm, down-to-earth barn spirit.*

# A STONE BARN RENEWED

After spending many years living and working in cities throughout the U.S., the LeHanes were lured back to Virginia, home of their college alma mater. The locale of Glenfiddich Farm suits the LeHanes to a tee. Lou is an international business consultant and likes having Dulles Airport just a 20-minute drive away. Janet runs a small antiques business, and the Leesburg area is a mecca for antiques buffs. But business considerations and convenience aside, the couple loves Glenfiddich for the gracious living it affords.

The main core of the born-again barn is a magnificent 14x31-foot great-room, shown here and on page 208. Featuring a 21-foot-high vaulted ceiling, a hayloft-turned-gallery, and beautiful old pine floors, the combination sitting/dining room exudes one-of-a-kind personality.

Upon entering the room, it's immediately apparent that the LeHanes are avid collectors. No matter where the eye travels, there's something of interest to see. Lou's passion is collecting duck decoys, and many of his favorite specimens are

decoratively perched on the ceiling crossbeams (see page 208). Other cherished finds include antique carousel figures, weather vanes, and an extensive collection of blue-and-white china dramatically displayed in the dining area, *opposite.*

Adding to the enchantment is the exciting juxtaposition of refined colonial furnishings placed in a rustic setting.

■
**Gracing this end of the great-room is a whimsical weather vane and a charming array of antiques.**

■
**On display in the dining area is a magnificent collection of antique china from the Ching dynasty.**

BUSSELL & WESTON CO.

# A FANCIFUL COTTAGE

**T**his exceptionally charming house is a fantasy come true for owners Tina and Bob Patterson. Says Tina of her enchanting cottage, "Not only does it look like the house of my dreams, it *feels* like it, too—romantic, fun, and lighthearted."

Tina's image of a storybook house stems from memories of her grandmother's country house, childhood fairy tales, and a trip to England. "The first time I saw a turreted Cotswold cottage, I knew I had to have a turret on my house," says Tina. Now, thanks to an artful remodeling project, her wish has become a reality.

■ With its English-cottage exterior, this West Coast home exudes a special kind of charm.

■ In true fairy-tale fashion, the cottage is approached through an ivy-covered, painted garden gate.

213

# A FANCIFUL COTTAGE

To exact maximum character from the modest cottage, the Pattersons sought—and found—a builder/designer who said "can do" when presented with a just-a-dream plan. Explains Tina: "Other builders and architects thought we were crazy when we said that a turret was a top priority. What we needed was a kindred spirit, and fortunately, we found one."

The new turret forms a much-needed entry hall, to the left and right of which are the remodeled living and dining rooms. Here, new custom-made French doors and gracefully arched Palladian windows fill the once-dark rooms with sparkling light. And to ward off darkness on cloudy days, Tina painted both rooms an exuberant shade of yellow. Furnishings are an artful blend of personal treasures—auction buys, heirlooms, and cherished paintings by Bob's father.

■ **Painted yellow, the coffered ceiling is a standout feature of the living room.**

■ **The dining room's new architectural assets include gracefully arched windows and an elegant fireplace.**

# A FANCIFUL COTTAGE

Conveniently located on the first floor of the house, the Pattersons' newly added master bedroom features French doors (behind the chair, *opposite*) that open, cottage-style, to a lovely garden patio. When the weather permits, Bob and Tina drink their morning coffee alfresco, but on cold or rainy days, a bay window sitting area, *below right,* offers a pleasing indoor alternative.

The slender writing-cum-dining table is an old family piece, and the open-arm chairs were purchased used from a friend. Just beyond the sitting area lie new his-and-her baths and dressing rooms—luxuries that were added as part of the general remodeling.

To visually meld the bedroom with the garden outside, Tina used a pretty floral print fabric for the draperies, bedspread, and seating pieces. She also embellished the fireplace with a simple floral design worked in hand-painted tile. Peach-color walls and a soft peachy-pink carpet echo hues found in the fabric.

Like the rest of the house, the master bedroom is filled with personal references. When Tina was a child, she longed for a dollhouse and a four-poster. Now she has both. The stately bed is a spindle-post heirloom from her grandmother's country house, and the whimsical dollhouse—Tina explains with a smile—is "a special gift from me to me."

For comfortable fireside seating, Tina added a small-scale rattan lounge chair and matching ottoman—the only contemporary influences in the otherwise traditional setting.

■
**Tina romanced the new master bedroom with garden colors and generous amounts of floral fabrics.**

■
**The bay window area is a perfect place for sipping morning coffee.**

# CREDITS

# CREDITS

## Field Editors

Our thanks to the following *Better Homes and Gardens®* Field Editors for their valuable assistance in locating many of the homes featured in this book.

Patricia Carpenter &
    Associates, Ltd.
Barbara Cathcart
Eileen Deymier
Carolyn Fleig
Estelle Bond Guralnick
Sharon Haven
Emily Kamatos
Bonnie Maharam
Ruth L. Reiter
Maxine Schweiker
Mary Anne Thomson
Jessie Walker Associates

# INDEX

# INDEX

# INDEX